Secrets of Weather & Hope

Sue Sinclair

Secrets of Weather & Hope

Brick Books

NATIONAL LIBRARY OF CANADA CATALOGUING IN PUBLICATION DATA

Sinclair, Sue, 1972–
   Secrets of weather & hope

Poems.
ISBN 1-894078-15-2

I. Title. II. Title: Secrets of weather and hope.

PS8587.I55278S42   2001   C811'.6   C2001-930377-7
PR9199.3.S5342S42   2001

We acknowledge the support of the Canada Council
for the Arts for our publishing programme. The support of
the Ontario Arts Council is also gratefully acknowledged.

The cover photograph, 'Torbay Clouds', is by Peter Sinclair.

Typeset in Bauer Bodoni; the stock is acid-free Zephyr
Antique laid.

Brick Books
431 Boler Road, Box 20081
London, Ontario   N6K 4G6

brick.books@sympatico.ca

For Mum, Dad, and Steve

Contents

Household Effects

The Pitcher 11
Collar Bones 12
Green Pepper 13
Peonies 14
The Dorsals 15
In the Bathroom 16
Navel 17
The Least Terns 18
Calcareous 20
Tulips 21
A Single Piece of Wood 23
Red Pepper 24
Lilies 25
Upstream 27
Bone 28

Galleries

André Kertész 31
Bach's Concerto for Harpsichord in F Minor 32
Four Poems for Virginia Woolf
i Portrait 33
ii A Sunday Drive 34
iii Observation 35
iv The Pattles 36
Learning the Waltz 37
Lyric Strain 39
Stained Glass 40
Doorways 41

In the Diner   42

Orange and Red Streak by Georgia O'Keeffe   43

Frobisher Bay   45

Aperture   48

Toronto Skyline   49

Trestlework   50

Clouds

Meteorology   53

Stratus   54

Cumulus   55

Cirrus   56

Altocumulus Undulatus   57

Cirrus Radiatus   58

Thunderhead   59

Thunderhead II   60

Orographic Clouds   61

Contrails   62

Stratocumulus Undulatus   63

The Absence of Clouds   64

The Hours

Mid-Afternoon   67

Six O'Clock   68

Seven O'Clock   69

Eight O'Clock   70

Café Interior, Night   71

Twelve O'Clock   72

Domestic Habits   73

Naming the Lilies, You Sleep   74

Saturday Afternoon   75
Springtime   76
The Scent of Wolf Willow   77
March   79
August   80
Saskatchewan   81
Grazing   82
Heat Effects   83
Concessions   84
Departure   86

Household Effects

The Pitcher

Unafraid of the dangers
of perspective, of distance,
round as a fruit, sure
of its proportions,
it confides in us its secret:
an inch tall, an inch around,
dainty lip and handle
ready to pour.

You want to hold it in your hand
because it fits, and makes you believe
in a place as small and certain
as that, like the way we remember
childhood
            through a keyhole:
our tiny mother,
tiny father, the tiny bed
in which we slept. Did we dream?
We did not. The sun rose
again and again, digging up the day.
Endlessly we began. Our cheeks were rosy.
We cried tiny tears.

The pitcher shines, the persuasive
curve of its body leads you
into recollection. So small
there's no room for doubt.
But what doubt did you have? Some things
you never quite forgot, and some
you always believed were true.

Collar Bones

Why do they make us think
of birds, the spreading of wings?

Only the mind is more in love
with flight. Desire

rises, hinges at the throat:
here is where we glimpse

one another, in the aerodynamics
of bones that skim the neckline, glide

from shoulder to shoulder, two halves
of a single bone healed

separately. Through us
they wish for a lost

amplitude, hint at a symmetry
that might have been.

Green Pepper

Glossy as a photograph, the bent
circumference catching
the light on its rim. Like a car's
dented fender, the owner desperate
to assess the damage, unable
to say, like the sun, *it can't
be helped.*

Conspicuous and irregular
all its life, born
with its eyes shut tight,
as though there really were a collision
it was trying to avoid. But it hasn't
happened yet – there is only
the impact of light: it has never

been in love, never drifted apart,
never fantasized about another
fragrant vegetable, never
been flattered, never been denied,
never wanted more than it has.
A life governed by absence:

the gleam of white
on its hollow body.

Peonies

They've taken it too far
and no one can bear it.
A cheap display – they'll do anything
for attention. But they've grown
past the point of frivolity, drooping
under their own weight, the petals so many,
so splendid, they force you to look
into the place where colour
submerges, gives itself up, and you might
find out what you're willing to risk.

They were convinced this needed to be
done. They have laid their heads down
for it. You feel some regret: the petals
are so red. The rain scatters them so.

The Dorsals

Theirs the most domestic
of tasks:
   the shifting of weight.

They live under the harness,
get the job done; these

are the muscles
with which we bear
death, dirt, loss.

They seek no explanation.

In the Bathroom

faucets lean
over the basin
    stretch their necks
    a pair of mated birds

the world falls into long shapes
inside them
    colours from shower curtains and
        geraniums caught   in the bones
        in the heart

the tap on the left
carries
a chain of
   drops (irregular)
      drops
  in its mouth
      puckers just where the water
breaks off and
    ends in streaming
        darkness

                the tap on the right
                  shines in three places
          a gleam   on its neck
          near its base
                      and
                  one in the crown
both throw cold
      and clear-striking
notes

into the basin below

Navel

curled hand, eye
of violin, head of fern

thimble, flower opening
or closing, pale skein,
coiled snake, twist
of lemon in gin, periwinkle

anything that concentrates,
that can set itself
on fire, that can spin
a cocoon
        a galaxy winding
into itself:
anything that disappears

The Least Terns

*'What interested me most ... was the manner in which the birds
had decorated their nests.... Here and there along the beach, the
'leasties' had picked up flat bits of sea shell about the size of a
finger nail, and with these bits they had lined their nest, setting
the flat pieces in flat, like parts of a mosaic.'* – Henry Beston

When the sky finally falls
only the tiniest tern will remember
what holiness is: a flower
in mosaic at the bottom
of his nest. As storm after storm
rages he flies through the eye
of the needle
into a seamless place with a cracked

scalloped shell in his beak, drops it
into the nest, a shallow bowl
of mussel shells, moon shells, clam shells
chalky pieces softened
by water, like the look
on your face when you wake up and discover
you are at home.

The tern's eggs lie bare
on the shore, this open cradle full
of open cradles. Sand rips
the air. You'd think the eggs
would be blown away, smashed
when everything around them seems
to have cracked, but they,
in these wild days
before sleep, know something
of life on a shelterless beach

and keep themselves
quietly to themselves.

Calcareous

for David

I wish I were as still
as you. A moon shell
left by the tide, its soft and faceless
face. Like you it intends nothing,
doesn't comment on the light
but absorbs it. Chalked in, almost featureless,
only when you turn it over does its mouth open
wide and submissive. That incorruptible pink
clearly mineral, like feldspar.
But you can only see in so far.
The last recess is inhabited
by emptiness, a curve
that cannot be seen.

Tulips

so yellow they inspire
confidence, we believe them
when they say
     they will always be
just so
and wish we could be too

the persistence
of this yellow
     its autonomy
like something dreamed up
by an ad agency, the desire
it manufactures
     in full colour
it presents itself
as immutable
like dishes or cutlery

so we buy the tulips and arrange them
in a jar, sprinkle a little sugar
in the water
     almost superstitiously

they are like goldfish: everything exposed
immobile, paralyzed
     not by stage fright
but by the implicit strength
of colour, too much
to live up to

and slowly, over a week, a week
and a half, the petals become

translucent
            acquire
the shininess of ill-health

we can't help
but be disappointed, should have known
but the heart escapes us

            it closes, opens
closes, opens and opens and
lets the petals go
            gives up the pretence

why, we ask

did we expect
so much of it?

A Single Piece of Wood

it seems in need
of consolation, its long neck
against the shoulder
                      the cello
wistful despite its size
has the curve
of a wishbone

you can't wander off like you can
with a violin, must stay faithfully
put
       but it feels your desire
to leave sometimes,
            it gazes outward
its polished face
a single piece of wood split
open to reveal the heart –

considered seriously
even the elbow
becomes desirable, inclined
to moments of amorous intent

the bow drags itself
across the hollow:
                  all is not lost
the cello's woeful body
sends out halo after halo

Red Pepper

Forming in globular
convolutions, as though growth
were a disease, a patient
evolution toward even greater
deformity. It emerges
from under the leaves thick
and warped as melted plastic,
its whole body apologetic:
the sun is hot.

Put your hand on it. The size
of your heart. Which may look
like this, abashed perhaps,
growing in ways you never
predicted.

It is almost painful
to touch, but you can't help
yourself. It's so familiar.
The dents. The twisted symmetry.
You can see how hard it has tried.

Lilies

I

The callas, stylish
as the waved hair of women
who do lunch, picking at shrimp
over white tablecloths.
They leave the tails on the edge
of their plates, implying
that they have done this before, many times,
and don't even think of them
as tails anymore. It's a matter
of decorum, a neat snip
of the teeth. The waiter removes the plates.

II

That desire both
to be touched and not to be touched
quite yet. Inchoate even as they turn
their heads, hoping to be seen. They remind
you of adolescents, a single whorl
curled over at the edges, revealing
just enough to make you want
a way in, while it carries you around
itself, abandons you on the periphery.
You lose sight of where you are,
where you want to go; there is nothing
but this beginning.

III

Napkins drape across
the women's laps: the centre crease
is still visible, hinting
at the immaculate, at how quickly
they could be refolded and how clean
they will always be – so they think, and go on
thinking even after the women dab their lips
and go. All the women leave them like this,
carelessly crumpled. They have learned
that to remark on anything is to draw attention
from themselves. There is no mystery
to this; the flowers on the table
have figured it out: they won't tell you
anything you want to know.

Upstream

Pouring over the weir, the river
is time reversing. The trout that flash
silver out of the water are splitting
seconds, infinitely, until the fragments
are so small you can't see them, invisible
flicks of light from their tails.

We aren't prepared for how myopic
they are, nosing at the falls, looking for a way
in. A leap, we say, expecting
a beginning and an end, but as long
as they hang there they are not made
of time. They do fall back, but
however briefly, the moment opens
up for them and they pass through,
even those who miss the mark
entirely – those perfect, useless arches.

Bone

It is winter.
The room is white.
Do not strain your voice.
We can make do.

Light is hard and clean
but not unsparing
as we had thought.

The angels have not
forgotten. Close your eyes.
You have gotten used to silence.

Galleries

André Kertész

about the light all
I can say is how it surfaces,

                    makes bare,
how nothing knows itself, the tulip
in its vase, opening,
       the railing which leads neither
up nor down but waits,
drowsy;
things are like this sometimes, indoors,
mid-afternoon,
               every lit form proposes
not just the doing but the falling
into doing
            – ah, so it has happened
at last, the tulip,
              marooned
in its own vastness, complicates nothing

Bach's Concerto for Harpsichord in F Minor

No hurried scattering of notes
instead
      music that requires the minimum
of motions, with room for sadness to roam
like the moon
           aware of brevity –
                 washing,
stroking your lover's hair, closing
or opening a door: a single task
completed
      so slowly it seems
something is breaking down. Between
each pause you could die
or come back to life, and it must be
one or the other. We have
entered an unused room; dust drifts
through a shaft of light
and it isn't
laziness but something more
deliberate:
      think of
the moon's circle, domestic
work, some bare vestige
of motion,

a music that doesn't ask
you to sit still, not
         quite.

Four Poems for Virginia Woolf

1 Portrait

Too much forehead. In photographs
she always looked sad. It should have been easy:
to sink to the bottom of oneself,
to be like sleep. But the thought of her own face
haunted her. She couldn't forget. The man staring
from under the dark cloth.

She couldn't sleep either: *good night, bad night, fairly*
good night:
          Leonard's diary,
Sinhalese and Tamil characters
intricate as the bones
in the ear. A cryptic alphabet
from his days
in Ceylon, coiled letters winding
into themselves, a glimpse
of madness. What her thoughts
might have looked like.

From the camera: quizzical
brows, aquiline nose.
Her eyes, sometimes, and the weight of water
behind them.

ii A Sunday Drive

'Of course you know the Goat is mad.' – Vanessa Bell

the piece of her that kept
breaking down, breaking down
like an old car, the one you know is going
to sputter, backfire, and leave you stranded
in the country, again, but you drive it
because it's yours, and you know
the clutch, how it gives, gives out,
and retains a certain
fatalistic charm

Of course it was more serious
than that – more than a flat tire, someone
trudging off in the dust. You can't help
but be flippant between times. A kind
of forgetfulness that lets you make light,
make love, make the drive
into the country. To talk
as though it were nothing.
To picnic and look at the hills.

iii Observation

she doesn't imagine it:
they stare when she passes,
can't help themselves, giggle
at the sight

there is something amphibious
about her: all eyes and faintly
ridiculous in cloche hat
and woolen coat, stepping out
to tea at Charleston
                       a caricature
the frog-lady shuffling
along, a lily-padded gait

who knew she noticed?
she never blushed, never looked up
but she doesn't know why
they nudge each other, dreams
she is naked and wakes up
sweating

she looks in the glass
and there it is, the trace
of her ancestors
half bone, half
                     cartilage
mutant limbs, transparent lids
and open, open eyes

iv   The Pattles

Seven beautiful sisters, your mother's
great-aunts, a legacy
of bone structure. Arm in arm they step out
of the last century, turning heads
in every decade. They emerge
in your mother's face, the grace of her brow,
a perfect oval. A madonna, they said,
a saint. The angel in the house.

You are not your mother – they say this to you
when she is gone. But you knew it, you knew
because of the parties, how everyone
fell in love with her, revealed themselves –
not secrets but things they told
no one else. You did it too. No, you are
not your mother. No *boeuf en daube*.
You haven't got her knack for opening doors,
those lovely cheekbones, that skeleton key.

Whether or not to try it. To pull out the best
china, order the roast, and – then what?
You can't feel it as she did, seating them
around the table. Even the candles
won't light properly, cast the right shadows.
Their faces are dim; the room empty.

Learning the Waltz

1

Is the war over yet?

whispered through static, faint
and unfamiliar voices, holdouts: crouched and dusty
orchestras scratch out old tunes, ghostly
patterns chalked onto the floor (box, circle, Viennese,
Blue Danube, Merry Widow, Skaters, Londoners,
Sugar Plum Fairies). But the needle
skips; the steps collapse,
stuttering. Chalk marks erase. The instruments
are taken away, lifted
from the turntable and confined to bedrest
and old age. Violin strings come loose, the heavy-bottomed
cellos dodder off.

2

Perhaps we feel we've outgrown
the waltz, its bent for the obvious. The simple
three-count, gauche, beckoning to first-time slow-coach
dancers. A more even time signature is preferred
without the irreducible fraction
of three-four time, its
                              asymmetrics;
the third beat that catches
us off guard. An extra heartbeat slipped in, it
refuses the drop, stays us a moment

before the musical ground
shifts. We lose our footing, fall
through the lost fourth
beat, get caught up again

                    by one.

3

As creatures of time and space
this is our number. It confounds us.
We count our way around the room. Rhythm
transforms the landscape; walls rear up
unexpectedly. The floor tilts
and we falter: this can't be how
it was done. Everywhere we look
the laws of angles revise themselves.
Space has never been more three-dimensional.

Lyric Strain

The hum of bees. How it unnerves us: we tremble
when a tree branch bends too low. The din
of traffic is almost more bearable than the garden
where a hungering quiet erupts from the roots,
cell by vivid cell.

A bee hovers near, quivers in the shadow
of the ear. We stiffen, scared it might drop
inside and set our bones ringing. The sound is after all
not too large but too small: a resonance our skulls
can't bear. What we feared wasn't the great brightness
but the minute trembling
of tiny hairs, that shiver of recognition.

Stained Glass: *Autumn Landscape,*
Tiffany Studios, New York, 1923

because sometimes the world
is like this, fuelled by light,
each leaf's turning transparent
as the eyes of saints

glazed over not because
they are bored, or there is nothing
left to do,
but because there is this:

you would swear
every restaurant, every shop, every glossy
magazine in New York City
photosynthesizes, works out the delicate
equation between life and

red is the colour of
        blue is the colour of
                green is the colour of

the trees who, monk-like, have given
everything away; we see through and through
until there is nothing left
but light
        on the far side of things

Doorways

from *Interiors* by Woody Allen

everything seen in a barren
light, the human face
looking for itself, wishing
for that openness,
                    doors left ajar
what else can be said
about a room, its occupants,
it doesn't matter
                    there is a doorway
and even that is brief, unconversational,
never enough happiness,
enough loneliness
to account for it all, what little comfort
comes, perhaps a vase though no flowers
in it yet *I wouldn't mind,* she said,
except
          her eyes look up
and we imagine we might refuse
to cry,
          see something
that will change our minds

In the Diner

white teacups
fill the air

spoons tap on rims openings
    gleam
        in every conversation

rounded tips touch the bottoms
of bowls
        find each other
over tabletops

a community of cups
halos shining here
                    and there
and here again,
reassuring the many
            the massive
the odd-figured hands
encircling them

everyone needs
this pittance of birds
that won't
            fly away

cups filled
with tepid water
each

a weighted bell,   a tiny earth-bound
        heaven

Orange and Red Streak by Georgia O'Keeffe

If everything really did begin
as light. Then slowly filled the need
for flesh, for sweetness of bearing.

Oranges, pears, green apples
leaching inward, bleeding
internally. Firming up.

If a nectarine grew
from the outside in, it would look
like this. Fist of light
moulded onto darkness, darkness
like a last. Red hills in the distance.

Yellow accumulating weight
becomes orange. The belly of fruit
ripens: let us not forget then

the shrinking darkness, the hand
on the back of its neck, forcing it
down. Bullied into the centre
it crouches in a shrivelled
almond. Think of its frustration
when you bite in, interrupt
the meditation –
a nectarine concentrated
on compactness. On the face of it
there seems to be no thought
more pressing than the sky

but it has bled itself into being
and nothing wells up inside it
and nothing wills itself to grow.

Frobisher Bay

In 1578, Martin Frobisher planned to establish a colony on Baffin Island and brought with him a stove covered in decorative ceramic tile. Archaeologists have since unearthed fragments of tile from the abandoned site – the fragments show two allegorical figures, one of which is Hope, the other Logic. Tiles have also been found at Innuit sites.

I

Hope: her voluptuous body, the virtues
of her anatomy – breasts artfully
concealed by a well-placed arm. All eroticism
sotto voce, eyes uplifted, averted from
her sumptuous belly, her swelling thighs.
She is scrupulously
unclothed. Naked as a child
is naked. As a bulb is
under the snow.

II

What does Hope do, left in the Arctic?
Eyes still open, ecstatic,
still gazing up, snow-blind perhaps.
She waits. Ice jams, ice floes,
moulting birds in spring
and still no one comes
to break camp. She dreams
of London and palaces, a warm stove,
china, Elizabeth's hands.
There's nothing for her to do here.

The continued twilight. The sun
that never quite disappears.
She waits for her gentleman explorer
to take her home.

III

What about her wings?
Useless. Absurd. Stubby
appendages for corpulent
flesh. Like a dodo, grounded,
a stutter as close
as she could come to lifting off.

Logic, ashamed of her own disproportionate
wings, sits quietly in a corner
and calculates the mass required
to fly home. Hope does nothing,
doesn't believe in folly.
She believes in flight
just as she believed it really was gold
he had found, and that he would
be back.

IV

They found her in relief, body
pressed onto clay tiles. Curious,
they touched her smooth belly,
fat as a seal, blubbery.
They brought her home. Taught her
how to skin a cariboo, make slippers
from bird skin, use sinew
for thread. She grew skilful,
practical. When the archaeologists
retrieved her, her edges were worn
smooth. She looked at their familiar faces
with glazed eyes.

Aperture

for Neil

It's all about chance – how it moves you.
The people you meet, what you say
to them, letting them hold the camera
if they ask. How they respond.

You have this effect on people. They wait,
more patient than they have been
all their lives. They pull themselves
together, not quite understanding
what will happen next, but eager
for it. A chance perhaps
to make good, to face what has become
theirs: what they think of the dead.
The things they saw as children.

The flash, when it finally comes,
picks it up faintly: a blur, the virga
behind the eyes – rain that evaporates
before it hits the ground. Weather,
time, their uncertain recovery.

Toronto Skyline

Nothing to cast a shadow
up there, buildings pale
and glittering, fascinated
by themselves and a little
ashamed. Far back in their minds
they know they have arrived empty-handed
but pretend they're not yet
where they want to be, wherever
that is. Sometimes, watching a pair
of starlings swoop and duck, they almost
admit it, give in to doubt. A kind of vertigo.
It's the heat, we say, that makes them
waver, and they ignore it too, wait
for it to pass. Be taller,
they say to themselves,
be taller, because that is the only way
they know how to think.

Trestlework

These bridges,
their susceptible arches,

the way they swell
in the middle
like a heartbeat
       spooning:

they shouldn't be
visible, architectures
of longing, chance

sightings: desire
emerges in scaffolds, music
tricked out of the minds
of engineers.

They rise publicly, aching
with effort, to risk everything –

each rod, linked
to possibility, strains
for an extra inch
       from the ground,
imagines itself
a framework for flight.

Clouds

Meteorology

We long to rise into the clouds
above mountains, don't think
of freezing, or how long we would last
if we were carried up.

Blue lips and cheekbones, eyelids
blue and closed against the cold.
Frost in the lungs, in the liver.
White hands. White fingers. White
or blue, either way, it's too pale:
we would fade into the clouds,
become heavy with rain, rain
and be done. A certain tenderness
might linger below

as it often does after rain.
Someone might recognize it.
Someone who loves you
might look up.

Stratus

They come as close
to us as sleep, leaving
heaven behind. Only the palest halo
stays around the sun –

                    a reminder.
If we were made of water
we might hover as they do, might be
as luminous. But they know
something of weight, an earthly
memory. You are tired
for no reason. You aren't really sure
you are awake. You feel far from home.

Cumulus

These are the carriers.
Their large, mild bodies make us think
of domesticity, of milk. Mammalian
they hold the rain in their bellies, a generous
temperament. They too are susceptible
to time, but more graceful than us.
Unafraid, they will let go
when they must. They breathe
more deeply and know something
of sadness. Their bodies are sympathetic.
Rain is what they know best and least.

Cirrus

To look up
all that distance
is to anchor yourself
more firmly to the ground.
It reveals the throat, curved
like a spoon. There, your heartbeat,
faintly visible. The less you
have the more it shows. Your face.
Your chin.

Wispy clouds, threadbare, traces
of things which have passed
effortlessly, without concern.
You look up through icy shades
of blue: there in the sky is the
thing you were about to say
and then forgot. Too high for memory.
Too high for rain. Nothing so remote
on Earth. The coldest, thinnest
part of you wants
to be up there, stillborn.

Altocumulus Undulatus

Too small to worry.
Asking not why
but when. A garden
of underdeveloped
shapes. Hydroponics
in the sky, vegetables
in their first flower:
white: albino squash,
starry-eyed cucumbers,
pea blossoms. They form
in regular rows, peer
down from the sky
wondering what they will do
when the time comes.

Cirrus Radiatus

'Radiatus have long, parallel streamers of relatively similar size that appear to converge toward the horizon.' – National Audubon Society Field Guide to North American Weather.

It makes you believe
you have come from somewhere,
let's call it *heaven:* a kind
of convergence, a distance impossible
to breach. Only the clouds
bring it near: perspective, a trick
of the light, infinity
a point on the horizon.
      Now we're sure
we can find our way and agree
to meet there, in the garden
we remember from the time before.
We will wait forever
if we have to, pluck apples
from trees, shuffle our feet
like angels do.

Thunderhead

Clarity: everything darker
and brighter. The ground smells
like water.

Thunderhead 11

An old movie: the light enlarges, turns the yellow
of a bruise, a pear. A grainy melodrama
that reminds you of the past. You sit back
and watch the sky eclipse itself, can almost hear
the reels creaking, feel the dusty light
over your shoulder. You are caught up, open-mouthed;
the plot develops. Rain for now
is an afterthought, a peripheral blur
on the bottom of the screen. What holds
your attention is the collision of clouds
overhead, opaque and fractured by light.

Orographic Clouds

Marble:
perhaps Michelangelo is still
at work. The sculpted curve
of an arm, a leg, appears unexpectedly
on the side of a mountain.
A tinge of homesickness: he misses
the Earth, can't stop wishing
he were back. The resemblance
is uncanny: looking up at
the contours of your own
body, you feel light-headed, distanced
from yourself. But it saddens you.
His restless devotion. This love
of bodies hanging in the sky.

Contrails

What is forgotten
is forgotten. We are already
off the ground, charging
through a vacuum, an inert sphere
once thought to be musical,
revolving.

Nothing left.
Look out your window:
it's too cold for music.
A tone deaf sky. We close
our eyes, try
to block it out. Plug into
classical or country. Lite rock. Behind us

a trail of ice. Particles
abandoned in the sky, miles away
from every life they have
known. They wait, suspended,
even their desire to melt
seized up. It's too cold
to want anything anymore.

Stratocumulus Undulatus

How the light cuts
through the atmosphere, falling
through dust, dust, dust.
In the time it takes
to reach the Earth, someone dies.

The clouds barely notice.
They think of the dead, the dying,
no more than of the light,
which slips through unremarked.
They have their own concerns:
soon it will be time to rain again.
They gather up water. They murmur.

The places where the dead
used to eat, sleep, love are like that space
between earth and sky. An empty room.
The mourners, looking up, see nothing.
Blind even when they shade
their eyes. Although the light opens
as it nears the Earth, breaking a little
to fall on them more gently, they still
don't understand. They see only the rain
that hasn't yet come – that and the light like a prism
in its strict cut, dividing, dividing.
They cringe as though it were an incision
in the heart, not the sky. They look down.
If only it had arrived sooner.
The light, not the rain.
It doesn't matter now when
it rains.

The Absence of Clouds

Look up and think of your mother,
your most distant memory.

Part of us dreads
blue. Cross your heart and give yourself

up: blue:
insufficient and miles away.

And yet you could swear you hear
something crying up there. You might

call it *forever,* and I suppose
the end could be more

like this: a brightness
that cleans you out.

Like the feeling of having
come through winter,

arriving one day
before spring.

The Hours

Mid-Afternoon

sometimes, when the light is right, it seems
all emotion can be reduced to a kind
of sadness
        an arthritic ache
welded into us, a keen bone
that seems to say
the same thing again
               listen:

light heaves itself
onto the city walls
       the rain has stopped
somewhere
a bird call –
         sound passed
through a prism, fractured
into its simplest
tones

Six O'Clock

stems of flowers
weaken, open mouths begging
the wind, the rain, the feet
of insects

to take the hearts
of their thin bodies
to another

that they might not
be left glutted,
splayed face-down
on a puddle

not even
enough time
    to sigh
and close

Seven O'Clock

forgetfulness
in the air
    we drift through drift
through pollen, like the mind
of an animal
as she lumbers home

bees worry the air, knot it
scurry over invisible
bridges
    their anxious, low-key
muttering shakes a single bone
inside the ear, tips
the balance
    we fall
against each other
pollen closes our eyes, wipes
the heart clean

Eight O'Clock

the air chills
toward dark, bees adrift and
sinking through moody drafts
        a hand unsure
whether or not to offer
itself, cool fistful
of light,
        a sheaf of wilted goldenrod
held out to an animal who leans her nose
over the fence and,
        reaching down, flares
her nostrils, blinks

Café Interior, Night

The windows become reflective,
forget the single thought
they acted out all day, letting time
pass. Now it doesn't exactly stand still
but seems to matter less, is less able
to come between us. The back of your head
merges with my shoulder
two tables away. Even our gestures
are continuous. Dark and light meet
and acknowledge one another,
strangers. Caught between panes of glass,
it's hard not to speak of ghosts. There
is little to fear in two dimensions, fewer ways
of being alone. Conversation has lost its urgency.
Something subterranean happens between us
and now talk is a matter of habit.

Twelve O'Clock

heat lingers
at midnight, an insect on the edge
of a finger, folding
and unfolding its wings

lilacs shiver, droop,
hang like caught breath;
abandoned gardening spades float
in mid-air, flowers, whole
houses buoyed up

bees are insomniac, can't resist
the pollen, how it bubbles up
in the dark
        the hum
of their wings interferes
with sleep, our bodies' burbling
dreams: we waken, sheets
knotted on the floor
      no one picks them up
instead we wait

for the unknown insect
to fly from the unknown
finger – for the bright
invisible flicker,

the thimble that drops
to the floor

Domestic Habits

The peculiar sadness when we watch animals
dream – does it awaken in us a travel
weariness, like the stars, part of that
distance, names silting
around our shoulders?

They are almost more familiar
asleep – a twitch, a low mutter
so much like worry you think
even they can't refuse insistent
thoughts, repetition – as if this
were something they didn't want
to admit: that they could easily
be like us. Though there's no proving it,
you are willing and fall for it. And just
when you're sure is when it becomes
hardest to bear:
                    that the hour changes
as they sleep, and when they wake up
they don't know what's happened
any more than we do.

Naming the Lilies, You Sleep

'... the gift

Of your small breath, the drenched grass
Smell of your sleeps, lilies, lilies.'
                    – Sylvia Plath. 'The Night Dances'

you lie face up
            as though
you have forgotten
to close

your eyes
thin-lidded
            your arm
veined and thornless

I wish I had something
to tell you
            think instead
of lilies of water quick
or slow

tiger arum rubrum
canna water I forget
the rest

you lie drenched in sleep
and on the pond of your inner
ear these names float
rootless

Saturday Afternoon

The somnolence of shoes
in shop windows; even the light
doesn't reach them, bounces off
and is escorted away before it can cause
embarrassment. There's no need
for a scene, a calm and plain refusal
is essential. Cool
and composed, they maintain themselves
in a dimly-lit interior, only half
thinking, giving merely the impression
of thought. Don't, they say, don't,
like all things behind glass. They look
over your head, purposeful, averted
gazes, as though seeing a brilliant
and hazy future you can't achieve
but might, if only they looked at you
that way. But you are fallible, you have loved
too much. There is nothing to be done
about this; you are too much like the light.

Springtime

The day has given up trying to be
anything in particular, imagines itself
in another place and almost believes it.
The clouds change shape quickly. They don't see
we can't keep up, how much slower
our hearts are. On a day like this
all you can do is keep pace with yourself.
You might be tired. So might everything else.

The flowers coming up in the gardens
open slowly, resistant to change. Drops
of water cling to the crocuses, the white petals
like a swan's oiled feathers. You feel sorry
for them, forget they know places
no one else goes. This memory is strongest
when they are open widest; they can disappear
just by thinking about it.

Behind a second-storey window a man
steps back from the light; shadows
fall over him like a hand
over a face. But it's just the clouds
reflected in the glass. It would never have occurred
to them to vanish. They know nothing will ever
be quite the same again. The sky meets your eyes
knowing next time it will reveal
as much and as little.

The Scent of Wolf Willow

Like honey
and nutmeg, fresh
baked cake with an extra ingredient
that threatens to drive you
wild with nostalgia:

you think of bees, a cloud
humming all around
without touching you, of kitchens
gone wild, gone native:
                    imagine
opening a cupboard
full of silver leaves,

imagine walking into your kitchen
to find it had vanished:

tarnished cutlery
spread on the lawn for days
afterward,

the fridge lying
under a tree, licking itself
clean.

Wolf willow: whistle
and it will not come; its tiny flowers
pretend not to hear; hidden in the cleft
between leaf and branch, they close
their eyes, hoping you will go
so they can go on remembering her,
the one they want,
the one who isn't home yet.

Easy enough to imagine
she won't come: the scent
is heavy, sinks quickly under
its own weight, more dense
than anything visible.

March

The car, cooling, ticks
like a cricket. Left
to itself it tries to forget
speed, come to grips with where
it wishes it came from: the green
middle of nowhere. At times
like this, a spring thaw,
all of us marooned on curbs
begin to think this way.

It pretends not to see itself
in puddles. Ignores chrome
and polish and thinks of a place
far away, a place so small
you could hold it in your palm, so complete
it could only have been imagined.
Ask your mother: there was never
a Sunday drive, no aunt or uncle
in the country. But what are you to do
when even the car remembers the green
sides of the road, the bright air,
how its pistons purred?
It is entirely convinced: as the heat
dissipates it feels its body
shrink and almost believes
it's going back.

August

Moist and warm, it makes newborns
of us all. Soft and pliant as leaves,
our systems drenched, lymph nodes
soaked. We could be springs, could be
rain, a source for the sky if it hadn't
already soaked up what it needs. Today
we don't have to give of ourselves
to repair the atmosphere, not a lung,
not a heart. We ascribe no motive
to the clouds. They are wet hammocks
slung close to the ground. We barely
turn in our sleep.

Saskatchewan

The cows have come
to see us, leaning
their soft, mucoussy noses
over the fence, their breath
heavy and smelling
of the ocean – salt, mollusc,
seaweed – it's not difficult
to imagine them, hooves and horns
rising out of the waves. Testing
their footing, they clomp
up the beach and wander
out to the prairie, looking for a place
to lie down. Their eyes show
how far they have travelled
but not what they have
seen. They have the look
of all lost peoples:
everything, even intelligence,
submerged, they peer
at us, wait for us to make
the first move. Only at dusk,
near the salt lick, do they
reveal themselves. We overhear
their rough tongues scraping
the block, as if that
were the way home.

Grazing

The prairie lies belly-up
in the sun, running
no risks: it has nothing more
to give up, nothing left to say.
It flourishes, literal, complete,
and doesn't resist the light:
you have travelled far, so have we all.
The flanks of the cattle shine
as they wander, heads down,
outcasts. There is no place
like home and it's useless
to search. No one could dream
anything stranger than belonging, a horizon
like this doesn't allow
for it. But it's as close
as you can get:

                    the grass
laying itself out, the distance,
the stubborn light, the cows
flicking their tails.

Heat Effects

The way we wait, in summer,
for the river to run dry, desire nothing

more than to unembrace ourselves
from gravity, to slip out from under

our animal pounds and ounces, burn up
our 65% water, even the tear ducts

parched. To have the thinnest
of arteries, a single-chambered heart,

small contracted lungs. To be the hollow
in bird bone, the condition for flight.

To be less, even, than this.
To be the step to one side, to let time
pass. To let memory migrate north.

Concessions

who would have thought the light
would affect us so –
   the disordering sadness
when it shifts
       not snow
but a certain
marrowless sky
says *winter*
       we begin
dying slowly, like plants, leaf
by leaf
   we say little
about it,
     conserve our thoughts
as a part of us remembers what it is
to starve

the day is too narrow
we hunch our shoulders

some slow down
some cry,
   forget
their maiden names
their home towns
    though no one asks

others become still
very still
      wish
darkness were longer,
its hollow to them
like the hollow of music
                  sometimes
they feel the tug of their hearts
on their bodies
     a slight sway
as the light vanishes

they look upon its disappearance
with no desire to go out
looking –
         it is enough
to know
it might not come again

Departure

Sometimes, autumn reveals the inward
light of things we call *glowing*.
A handful of red maple leaves.
A light that doesn't exceed itself
and has something to do

with departure. Think of a church,
the long, slow, sad colours, the way
they linger, miles from the sun, with no thought
of lingering. Again the red leaves.

Lay them on a table.
The dead have come back
to haunt the surface of the wood.
They can see themselves in the polish,
appear and disappear, something more than
and less than a face.

At the end of everything, you think,
there is this – this quickness,
this vanishing, this brilliance. The unseen
glimmer that bound it all together
escapes and is forgiven.

And everyone knows that forgiveness
gives off light, that healing
is the next thing to fire. It calls you
as it goes. You lay your
hand on the table.

Acknowledgements

For friendship and mutual support, thanks to:

Don McKay and Jan Zwicky for their time and attention
David Seymour
Eric Hill, Steve & Janet McOrmond, Murray Sutcliffe, Julie
Kerr, the Andies Weaver and Titus, Paul Dechene, Mike
Belyea, Shane Rhodes, Adam Dickinson, Michael deBeyer,
Eric Miller
Ross Leckie for his generosity
Sabine Campbell
everyone at the Ice House
everyone at the Nature Writing and Wilderness Thought
Colloquium – ticks excepted
everyone at Book City in the Village
Lisa Lindsay and Sophie Theriault for careful and astute
reading
Bruce Porter for early encouragement
and for even earlier encouragement: Mr Farewell, Claude
Schryburt
Cyril and Liliane Welch

Some of these poems have appeared in different versions in
*The Fiddlehead, TickleAce, The Malahat Review, The
Wascana Review, Canadian Literature, Prism,* and the
anthology *New Canadian Poetry* (edited by Evan Jones,
Fitzhenry & Whiteside, 2000). Thanks to all these
publications, as well as to everyone at Brick.

Biography

Sue Sinclair grew up in Newfoundland, went to university in New Brunswick and currently lives in Toronto. Her poems and short fiction have appeared in numerous Canadian journals and anthologies. This is her first book of poetry. She has completed a novel, *The Beekeeper's Daughter*.